To Cook
a
Bachelor's Goose

by Ruth G. Satzman

Illustrated by Harvey M. Knecht

GOLDEN PRESS NEW YORK

For Ben
Whose Goose
I
Cooked

Library of Congress Catalog Card Number: 69–18108
© Copyright 1969 by Western Publishing Company, Inc.
Printed in the U.S.A.
Published by Golden Press, New York

What's Cooking in This Book

C732016

Catch your bachelor with a winsome smile, and he'll resent the first frown you toss him. Corner him with clever chatter, and he'll be hopelessly bored when you're in your meditative mood. Wow him with a fabulous figure, and you'll panic if you gain a pound. But catch a man with creative cooking, and he's caught forever.

So if a day comes when you wonder why you aren't married, look in the kitchen, not the mirror. Then bait your own brand of tender trap with the recipes you'll find on the following pages. Each delectable dish is easy to cook, delicious to eat and very likely to succeed at man-catching. All can be cooked and served in small quarters. All are created to taste like they took endless hours to prepare, yet all are minimum time-consumers. Just follow the recipes carefully, season with your own charm, and your chances of carrying a bridal bouquet will soar.

To our mind, there's no magic in broiling a steak or chops. Besides, most men are well acquainted with this kind of cooking and can do it themselves. Wouldn't you rather cook your bachelor's goose with fresh thinking as well as flavorful food? Go ahead. Show him you have rare culinary talent.

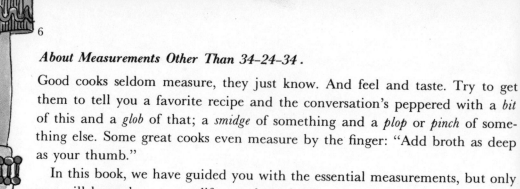

6

About Measurements Other Than 34–24–34.

Good cooks seldom measure, they just know. And feel and taste. Try to get them to tell you a favorite recipe and the conversation's peppered with a *bit* of this and a *glob* of that; a *smidge* of something and a *plop* or *pinch* of something else. Some great cooks even measure by the finger: "Add broth as deep as your thumb."

In this book, we have guided you with the essential measurements, but only you will know how to modify or adapt them to your own palate and his. As for the seasonings in general—often you'll notice that no amounts are indicated in the recipes. Use your judgment, but remember—better to err on the side of too little than to overseason and ruin the dish. Intuition and experience are the two best keys to culinary confidence.

The Salt of the Earth . . . And the Pepper

Spare the salt and save the dish! In many of the recipes, we have completely omitted salt so that the natural flavor of the food can be relished. Also, we don't call for monosodium glutamate or other flavor-accenting chemicals, but do use if you like. On the other hand, we enthusiastically hail freshly ground pepper. The initial purchase of a pepper grinder will more than pay off in flavor dividends for years to come.

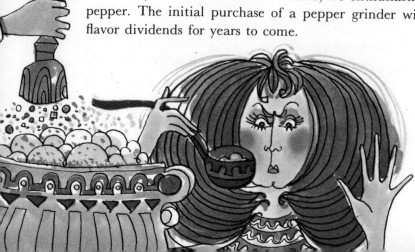

Read It Right

A word to the wise: Always read each recipe in the menu well ahead of time. More often than not, you'll find some helpful tips or instructions following the recipe ingredients. Also, as a double-check and for your own convenience, it's a good idea to assemble all the necessary ingredients before you start.

All of the recipes serve two unless we indicate otherwise. If you invite another couple to join you, just double the ingredient amounts. Or, by simple multiplication, you can also serve a crowd.

Before the Curtain Rises

When you're playing the hostess role, an electric hot tray is the best stage prop imaginable. It need not be an expensive, elaborate one. At this writing, an ideal size for the single girl costs about $18. With a hot tray on your table, you can cook everything beforehand and eliminate last-minute jitters. Your food will be kept warm and flavorful, ready to eat when you are ready to serve.

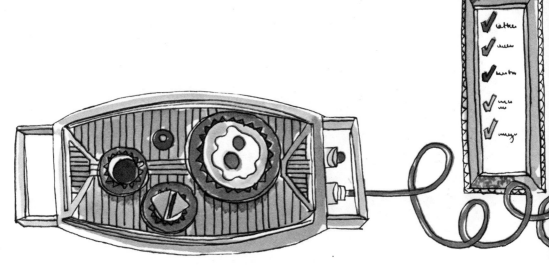

No-Dip, No-Drip Cocktail Party

or how not to put that man on the spot

Invite a number of eligible males, a few females, a happily married couple or two to illustrate how great things can be, and you're all set to corner the market. Just be sure to ask more men than women even if you have to dredge them up from the distant past. Be charming to all and don't pay too much attention to the man in mind. When it's time for goodbyes, if he offers to stay and help you tidy up—and only if—let him. The kitchen is a splashing place to bubble up a romance.

You should be the tastiest dish at your party, so don't overlook this opportunity to wear a long skirt, flattering hostess pajamas or elegant slacks. As far as the other snappy dishes are concerned, you'll notice all the hors d'oeuvre recipes are drip-free. Men hate messy dips; they spot suits and your furniture, too.

For the drinks, don't think for a minute that you need a complete bar set-up. No one expects it. If you have a good gin and a good vermouth, the Martini drinkers will be happy. Guests who prefer wine can have the vermouth, either straight or on the rocks. A name-brand Scotch will take care of whiskey imbibers. And for those who like a mixed drink, serve Whiskey Sours made with rye, lemon juice and sugar.

SALAMI ROLL-UPS . . . They get the party rolling

Ask your butcher to slice ITALIAN SALAMI paper-thin. Have him set the slicer at the thinnest possible setting even if some slices come out torn . . . and be sure he skins the salami before slicing. Wrap salami slice around spears of canned ASPARAGUS OR PICKLE SLICES. If salami is thin enough, the roll will seal itself. Figure on at least 3 or 4 of these roll-up combos per person.

PROSCIUTTO-MELON STICKS . . . Really hit the spot

Have the same butcher slice PROSCIUTTO (Italian ham) paper-thin. Cut slices of your favorite MELON into sticks about the size of asparagus spears. Wrap ham around the melon. Delicious! And different with drinks. Be sure melon is ripe. Buy it a few days before your party and let ripen in your kitchen. Do not refrigerate until ripe.

BACON-OLIVE DIVIDENDS . . . The pay-off starts here

Buy some LEAN BACON and some nice PIMIENTO-STUFFED OLIVES. Cook the bacon until half done. Wrap a bacon slice around each olive and fasten with a toothpick. You may not need an entire slice of bacon per olive but be sure slice overlaps. (Save any leftover bacon for tomorrow's breakfast.) After your guests have arrived and the party needs warming up, pop your pan of bacon-wrapped olives under the broiler just long enough to crisp bacon. Serve sizzling hot.

MINI FRANKS . . . All eyes are on the dogs

Men always like little frankfurters, so make yours extra-special this way: Buy TINY ALL-BEEF FRANKFURTERS (about 25 or 30 to the pound). Heat slowly in the oven or broiler. Meanwhile, in a saucepan, mix 1 tablespoon of CORN-STARCH, ½ cup of BROWN SUGAR, ⅓ cup of VINEGAR, 6 tablespoons of PINEAPPLE JUICE and 2 teaspoons of SOY SAUCE. Bring to a boil, and simmer until it is a heavy sauce. Add the warm hot dogs. Serve in a chafing dish.

‛PICY MEATBALLS . . . Now you see them, now you don't

You can make these in the morning on the day of your party, but don't put them in the refrigerator. Keep them over the pilot light on your stove or in the oven, and just before serving heat them up. Here's the recipe—a flavor surprise men will like.

For 68 meatballs about ½ inch in size, use 1 pound of LEAN GROUND CHUCK, 1 EGG, 1 large ONION, chopped fine, SMOKED SALT and GARLIC POWDER. Brown onion in VEGETABLE OIL OR MARGARINE. *Lightly* mix the browned onion and everything else with the ground meat. Use your own judgment about the amount of salt; a good teaspoon gives a nice smoky flavor. Trust yourself with the garlic powder, too.

Form the balls with a delicate hand; don't pack them hard. Brown over medium heat in the same pan you used for the onions. If necessary, add more oil or margarine. Swoosh the balls around in the pan occasionally so that they're nicely browned all over. Sprinkle in a few drops of WORCESTERSHIRE SAUCE during cooking. Don't overcook—you want them soft and juicy.

When it's warm-up time, spill enough CHILI SAUCE into the pan to coat it; add the meatballs and place over low heat until thoroughly hot. Serve in a chafing dish over an alcohol or Sterno burner, or a candle warmer, or on an electric hot tray. Do keep them hot. Be sure there is a little container of toothpicks so guests can help themselves easily.

STEAK TARTARE . . . Raw deal for tigers

Ask the butcher to grind 1 pound of ROUND STEAK. (Don't, don't buy it prepackaged. The meat must be freshly ground.) Place the meat in a mixing bowl. Break in 1 EGG. Give your PEPPER grinder a few strong twists. Add SALT and very, very finely chopped ONION. Mix it all up, lightly but thoroughly. Spoon onto approximately 30 MELBA TOAST rounds or party RYE BREAD slices. Top each with an ANCHOVY, and just listen to your tigers roar approval.

CLAM-CHEESE SPREAD . . . Men really dig these clams

You'll need a 10½-ounce can of MINCED CLAMS and an 8-ounce package of CREAM CHEESE, about ½ teaspoon of GARLIC POWDER and a good squeeze of LEMON. Drain the clams and drink the juice. Now mix all the ingredients and spread on about 3 dozen MELBA TOAST rounds. Just before serving, run them under the broiler until very hot and a little bit brown.

DEVILISH EGGS . . . Innocent and irresistible

There's nothing unusual about deviled eggs, but they *are* easy, and men *do* like them. Here are some devilish good ways to do them for a change.

First, hard cook the EGGS by slipping them into BOILING WATER; lower heat and simmer for 20 minutes or more. Next, plunge into COLD WATER to keep the yolks from turning color (and also so you can handle them). Then peel. That's the proper way to do it. But you can also put the eggs in cold water and bring them to the boiling point; then turn the heat down and let them cook just below the boil for about 20 minutes. Cool in cold water and peel.

Cut eggs in half the long way. Remove yolks carefully into a bowl. Now you can start doing things like mashing them with . . .

MAYONNAISE, MUSTARD, SALT and PEPPER

TUNA FISH, SALT and PEPPER

MELTED BUTTER and CURRY POWDER

ONION (finely chopped and browned in melted butter), SALT and PEPPER

BACON (crisply fried and crumbled)

ROQUEFORT OR BLUE CHEESE

Then spoon any of these mixtures into hollows of whites. Top each with bit of PIMIENTO, a CAPER, a tiny PEARL ONION or sprig of PARSLEY. You'll notice we haven't told you the amounts of ingredients to mix with your egg yolks. Use your own judgment and the good taste will be there. Just be sure to mash until the mixture is smooth.

CHEDDAR CHEESE BALLS . . . What a great pitch

Little cheese balls make a big hot hit. You'll need: a cup of **BISQUICK**, ¾ cup of grated **SHARP CHEDDAR CHEESE**, ⅓ cup of **MILK**, a little grated **ONION** and some snipped **PARSLEY OR CHIVES**. Mix everything together except the parsley or chives. Form the mixture into ½-inch balls. Roll each in the chopped parsley or chives. Bake on a greased baking sheet in a 450° oven for about 10 minutes or less—watch your timing. Then watch your cheese balls disappear! This recipe makes about 25.

How will you grate the cheese and onions called for in this recipe? You can use a hand grater, but you'll be happier if you invest in a blender. It's not an extravagance; it's a good investment, and you'll use it often. You needn't buy an elaborate, expensive one that does everything but play "The Star-Spangled Banner." Buy the least expensive of the good brands. A two-speed blender is fine, and it will grate cheese beautifully. Never buy ready-grated cheese in packages. There's a sharp difference between packaged and freshly grated cheese.

CHEESE-STUFFED MUSHROOMS . . . Little runaways

Wash and dry 12 good-looking, medium-size **FRESH MUSHROOMS**. Remove the stems and put them in the refrigerator to use in another dish another day. Turn the mushrooms on their rounded backs. If they don't sit nicely, slice off a tiny bit to get a flat surface. Now take a 3-ounce package of **CREAM CHEESE** (room temperature) and season with **SALT**. Then mash with **CURRY POWDER OR GARLIC POWDER** or both. Or blend the cream cheese with **ROQUEFORT OR BLUE CHEESE**, in which case no other seasoning is needed. Fill mushroom hollows with the cheese mixture. Improve the view by capping the cheese with a touch of **PIMIENTO**, chopped **OLIVE OR CHIVES**.

Sunday Brunch

or how to get your bachelor to rise and shine in the morning

he really the man you want to breakfast with 365 days a year, plus one
y leap year? Find out. Invite him to brunch some Sunday and look at
in the light of day, away from the flattering shadows of those candlelit
ners.

Vhat you wear for that brunch should be as appetizing as what you serve
something he hasn't seen on dates or at the office. Crisp and gay are the
hwords here. And don't wear an apron—too much domesticity can
ten a man.

ecause bachelors come in assorted personalities, we suggest three different
ch menus keyed to three familiar bachelor types. Should your gentleman
rm to none of these categories, you're on your own. More fun that way,
way. But in any case, why not mix up the menus and see what happens?
may turn a lion into a lamb or coax a turtle to come out of his shell.

lan to serve everything graciously at the table . . . don't bring already-
d plates from the kitchen. You're his hostess and don't want to leave him
ne at the table for more than a minute or two. Feed his ego as well as you
d the inner man and you'll have him right where you want him.

or an added bit of elegance, serve **CHAMPAGNE** with any of these menus. And
ou decide to offer your bachelor a pre-brunch drink, make it a **BLOODY**
RY (tomato juice and vodka), a **BULL SHOT** (cold bouillon and vodka) or a
ODY BULL SHOT (tomato juice, bouillon and vodka). All are very simple to
ke and quite civilized for the mid-hours of the day.

Brunch For Bachelor A
Amiable, Attentive, Angers Slowly
. . . An easy catch!

SQUIRTLESS GRAPEFRUIT . . . Honey of a way to sweeten his day

Buy a *heavy* seedless **FRESH GRAPEFRUIT** (the weight tells you it's juicy). Cut it in half. Then cut all around the fruit and remove from shell. Keep the shell halves. With a serrated knife, cut each segment of grapefruit so there is no membrane surrounding the fruit. Drop sections into a bowl. Peel 2 juicy navel **ORANGES** and divide into segments. Mix with the grapefruit. Drizzle generously with **HONEY** and mix well. Spoon into shells; serve at room temperature.

CHICKEN LIVERS AND MUSHROOMS . . . Successful sorcery

Buy ½ pound of **FRESH CHICKEN LIVERS** and ¼ pound of **FRESH MUSHROOMS.** Wash mushrooms and cut off stem ends. Slice them the long way, keeping shape of mushroom. Wash the chicken livers and cut each in half with your kitchen scissors. *You don't have any?* They're a kitchen must—in many cases, much easier to use than a knife. Now cut off any clinging veins or bits of fat.

Melt about ¼ of a stick of **BUTTER OR MARGARINE** in a medium-size frypan. Toss in the mushrooms. Let them lavish in the melted butter over medium heat for a few minutes. Remove to a plate and deliver the livers to the same melted butter (add more butter if necessary). Just let them snuggle in the butter over medium-to-high heat. They should cook quickly. You'll know when they're done by lightly poking the largest liver with a fork, If no juice oozes, they are ready to be smothered with the cooked mushrooms. Sprinkle about 12 drops of **WORCESTERSHIRE SAUCE** over all and cover. Turn heat low and forget for a few minutes. Peek in a little later and if livers seem dry, moisten with about ¼ cup of **CHICKEN BOUILLON** (made with a cube and water).

CRAZY MIXED-UP SCRAMBLED EGGS . . . Sure to crack his reserve
For the two of you, crack 4 or 5 EGGS into a mixing bowl. Add 2 tablespoons of MILK OR CREAM, then a sprinkling of snipped FRESH CHIVES OR BASIL or a touch of OREGANO, or finely chopped CHEDDAR CHEESE. Or use *all* of them! Beat everything with a fork, wire whisk or rotary beater and pour into a frypan in which you've already melted about 2 tablespoons of BUTTER OR MARGARINE.

Turn the heat low and cook slowly, giving the cheese time to melt. With your spatula, push egg mixture away from sides of pan as it cooks, letting the uncooked part reach the hot bottom of the pan. Keep doing this until mixture is set but not dry or hard. As eggs cook and cheese melts, you can fold and shape the mixture as you wish. When done, remove to a heat-proof platter, surround with the chicken livers and put all on the hot tray. The food won't cook any more but will stay cozy and warm waiting for you and your bachelor.

HARMONIOUS ACCOMPANIMENTS

Serve him hot biscuits like mother never made. Buy ready-to-bake BISCUITS found in the refrigerator section of your market. Sometime during the activity of cooking the eggs and livers, preheat the oven as indicated on biscuit package. When the doorbell rings, pop biscuits into the oven. While you're arranging the flowers he brings, the biscuits will be baking. Place them in a basket or on a small tray and cover with a cloth to keep hot.

Oh, yes! . . . the COFFEE! We won't tell you how to make it; just be sure to have it ready when he arrives. Use your prettiest coffeepot and leave it on the hot tray to pour at the table when you wish. If you use instant coffee, never let him see the jar. You're not married . . . not yet anyway. You have a right to your little secrets.

Give him plenty of sweet treatment with small dishes of JAM, JELLY OR HONEY. And don't forget the BUTTER. Miniature DANISH PASTRIES to nibble with coffee are nice if you want to gild the lily.

Brunch For Bachelor B
Brainy, Benevolent, Bashful
. . . You'll have to overwhelm him!

MELON AND GRAPES . . . Cool little marriage

Buy your favorite type of MELON enough days in advance so it will be soft, sweet and perfectly ripe on the day of your brunch. Don't refrigerate it until ripe. Perhaps you need not refrigerate it at all; melon tastes sweeter at room temperature. Cut the melon in half or into wedges; scoop out the seeds. Put both portions in front of your place at the table along with a tiny pitcher of sweetened LEMON JUICE and a bowl of seedless GRAPES (washed and with stems removed). At the table, pour a little juice over melon and into the cavity. Fill cavity with grapes and pass, with a warm smile, to Bachelor B.

FRENCH TOAST AND CHICKEN . . . Smooth way to butter him up

Ask the butcher to bone and halve 1 large CHICKEN BREAST. Buy a loaf of UNSLICED BREAD, rich in egg. Slice bread into pieces about 2 inches by 4 inches, about ½ inch thick. Beat 2 EGGS with 2 tablespoons of MILK and a pinch of SALT. Dip bread into egg mixture and let it soak up a generous amount—give it a real egg-milk bath. Meanwhile, melt 2 tablespoons of BUTTER OR MARGARINE in your frypan. Sauté until golden on both sides. Allow at least 2 slices per serving. Place French toast on a platter; keep warm.

Take the 2 pieces of chicken breast, which you have washed and dried, and put them in the same pan with any melted butter that remains. Add more butter, if necessary. Sauté until deliciously firm and golden-white. Add chicken to the platter with toast and rush it to your hot tray.

Serve with MAPLE SYRUP or with MELTED BUTTER and CINNAMON-SUGAR. The only other thing you need is hot COFFEE and strong conversation.

Brunch For Bachelor C
Candid, Clever, Cantankerous sometimes
. . . He needs soothing

STRAWBERRIES OLE

Let there be no delay in feeding this man. When he arrives, have a small plate of whole **FRESH STRAWBERRIES** (unhulled) at each place. You've washed the berries carefully and drained off any drops of water. If berries are large, 4 or 5 per serving are enough. On each plate, have a tiny mound of **POWDERED SUGAR OR DARK BROWN SUGAR**. Take a berry by the stem, dip into sugar and pop into your mouth. If you wish, serve **ORANGE JUICE**, too.

FINNAN HADDIE POACHED IN MILK . . . A fine kettle of fish

This dish is really the salt of the sea and a great catch for brunch. It's already smoked, so cook without a trace of seasoning. Just cover a 1-pound piece of **SMOKED HADDOCK** with **COLD WATER** and bring slowly to a boil. Let it bubble for about 5 minutes. Drain off water, and cover fish with **MILK**. Again bring to boil; lower heat and simmer about 20 minutes.

Meanwhile, peel 8 tiny **WHITE POTATOES**; boil in **WATER** about 20 minutes. **SALT** *sparingly*. (Remember, the fish is already salty.) When potatoes are tender, drain and gently shake pan over heat to dry potatoes.

Drain off milk and place the finnan haddie on a platter. Surround it with potatoes. Sprinkle some snipped **FRESH PARSLEY** over the potatoes. Serve with a small pitcher of **MELTED BUTTER** and **LEMON WEDGES**.

With this brunch, **CORN MUFFINS** would be very nice. Have **JAMS, MARMALADE OR HONEY** to go along. The contrast of salt (from the fish) with the sweet is rather special so you don't need anything more except hot **COFFEE** and warm glances.

Saturday Lunch

or how to keep an eye on him when he's not working

He just won't think of inviting you out for Saturday lunch. Poor wifeless soul, his Saturdays are so filled with activity. He exhausts himself in the mornings gathering up his laundry or carting suits to the Bachelor's Friendly Valet Service. Or he's out on the golf course or playing tennis at an hour when he should be in the arms of Morpheus. Or he's schussing down the ski slopes, dazzling the bunnies along the way. (Come now, don't be jealous!) You'll just have to take the bull by the horns and introduce him to serene Saturday and lunch at your place.

Have some music playing softly when he arrives. Forget time; don't wear a watch. Do wear the prettiest daytime dress in your wardrobe so you're ready to out after lunch if he suggests it. But don't plan anything like a movie, or a play or concert. Just know what's playing where and what new shows have opened at the museums, galleries or whatever . . . *just* in case he asks. Your sole desire is to give him a lovely, leisurely lunch. (How you rushed around with *your* laundry and cleaning and cooking, he'll never know. But then, all in good time.)

Lunch For Mr. Amiable

. . . He's the dear with the peaceful personality; rarely anxious, seldom angry

SHRIMP, NEW ORLEANS STYLE

Cook this dish on Thursday or Friday—it tastes even better after a day or two in the refrigerator. Buy 1 pound of medium-size FRESH SHRIMP. Remove tails, shells and the black vein from back of each shrimp. Wash shrimp in COLD WATER. Ahhh! . . . Now the big part of the preparation is finished. (If you prefer, buy pre-cleaned and cooked fresh shrimp, or you can use the frozen.)

Peel 2 medium-size ONIONS, cut into thin slices and separate into rings. Chop 2 cloves of GARLIC very fine. Melt about 1 tablespoon of BUTTER OR MAR-GARINE with the same amount of VEGETABLE OIL. Sauté the onion rings and garlic until yellow and soft but not brown. Next, chop 1 large GREEN PEPPER into pieces about ½ inch square; mix with onions and garlic and sauté another moment or two. Then add a medium-size can of ITALIAN-STYLE OR STEWED TOMATOES.

Now's the moment for the seasonings of old New Orleans. The easiest way to capture this flavor is via a small jar of BOUQUET CREOLE, which you can find on the spice racks of many food stores; use about 1 tablespoon. If you're unable to find this conglomerate of spices, mix your own by adding generous pinches of CELERY SALT, CHILI POWDER, ONION POWDER, NUTMEG, GROUND CLOVES and PEPPER. Bring mixture to a boil; add the cleaned raw shrimp. Cook only until they turn a beautiful orange-pink, usually less than 5 minutes. And your dish is finished! If the mixture is thinner than you'd like it, add enough canned TOMATO PASTE to thicken. Let cool and refrigerate. When it's time for Saturday's lunch, heat mixture in the top of your double boiler, or warm slowly and carefully over direct heat.

RICE AND PEAS . . . Perfect shrimp mates

Your New Orleans Creole was made for rice and peas. Cook **RICE** according to the instructions on package, but instead of cooking in water, use **CHICKEN BOUILLON** made with water and a cube (1 cube to each cup of water). Don't worry your pretty head if every grain of rice isn't separated when cooked. As a matter of fact, sticky rice is very nice.

As for the peas: Use about half a 10-ounce package of **FROZEN PEAS** for the two of you. They need not be cooked. Simply put them in a heat-proof dish and let them relax over the pilot light of your stove for an hour or so. If you have an electric stove, use lowest degree of heat. When peas are defrosted and slightly warm, they're just right. Most people overcook peas to a soggy state. When the rice is finished, lightly mix in the peas. Place the hot Shrimp Creole in the center of a platter and ring it with the pea-studded rice. Deliver this delectable dish to your hot tray and serve at the table.

A green salad belongs with shrimp and rice. Serve your favorite crisp greens, dressed with one of the salad dressing recipes on page 38.

ABOVE PAR PARFAIT . . . A bogey on the last course

Since the shrimp is hot and spicy, serve a cool dessert. Make split-level parfaits in the morning and keep them in the freezer section of your refrigerator. They're so easy to make it's almost a sin for them to be so delicious and look so difficult.

In a parfait glass, footed wine glass or small goblet, cut up some **FRUIT**, fresh or otherwise, or use good **STRAWBERRY PRESERVES**. Spoon in some **ICE CREAM** and some more fruit and some more ice cream. It's also pretty to use various ice cream flavors and colors; or have ice cream at the lower level and **SHERBET** at the upper level. When you reach the top, a dollop of **WHIPPED CREAM** and a rosy **MARASCHINO CHERRY** (with its stem on) will add the artistic touch that intrigues the wariest bachelors.

Lunch For Mr. Bashful

. . . He's a whole refresher course! Hard to find, but easy to take
—a shining light who's never dull

SALAD WITH A FRENCH ACCENT

Traditionally called "Salade Nicoise," this type of salad is popular in Nice and much of Southern France. We've never had it the same way twice—in Nice or anywhere else. So here it is, in a fashion easy to assemble for an oh-so-chic luncheon on a Saturday après noon.

Tear washed-and-dried crisp LETTUCE into bite-size pieces. Add any or all of these fresh salad fixings: RADISHES, CELERY, CUCUMBERS, SCALLIONS (including green ends), GREEN PEPPER and rings of RED ITALIAN ONION. Flake a 7-ounce can of TUNA FISH into chunks. Toss in the tuna, PITTED BLACK OLIVES and PIMIENTO-STUFFED OLIVES, and ANCHOVIES, if you like them. Make a ring around the salad with HARD-COOKED EGGS and TOMATOES cut into quarters or eighths; 2 eggs and 1 or 2 tomatoes will do it. At the table, dress this super salad with OIL and VINEGAR and serve on large plates.

LAZY GARLIC BREAD

Use a small loaf of **FRENCH OR ITALIAN BREAD** or half a large loaf. Cut into slices about 2 inches thick, stopping the knife before you cut loaf all the way through; bottom crust should be solid. Place about 3 inches of a stick of **BUTTER OR MARGARINE** on a small flat plate. Sprinkle with about 1 teaspoon of **GARLIC POWDER** and mash until butter is soft and powder is well blended. Spread both sides of each slice with the garlic-butter, and place the loaf in a baking pan.

Heat oven to 450 or 500°. When your bachelor rings the doorbell, pop the loaf into the oven and *turn off the heat.* This way you won't have to worry about burning the bread, and when you're ready for lunch it will be hot and ready, too. Serve in a basket covered with a cloth to keep bread warm and irresistible.

Man may not live by bread alone, but you can butter up a bachelor very nicely by serving this Lazy Garlic Bread . . . and here are some equally delicious flavor twists. **LAZY HERB BREAD**—Mash the **BUTTER OR MARGARINE** with ½ teaspoon **SESAME SEEDS**, ¼ teaspoon **OREGANO** and a pinch of **THYME**. Spread and heat as above. **LAZY CHEESE BREAD**—Grate about 2 teaspoons **PARMESAN OR CHEDDAR CHEESE**. Mash with **BUTTER OR MARGARINE**. Spread and heat.

MAC SHERRY FINALE . . . **Powerfully romantic sparkle**

This salad lunch is so simple it calls for a very special dessert. Mac Sherry is just that. It tastes deliciously expensive, yet is anything but. If you're a thrifty lass, you can serve this to a whole clan at modest cost.

But for the two of you, break 8 **COCONUT MACAROONS** into small bits in a bowl. Pour a **MEDIUM DRY OR SWEET SHERRY** over the pieces. Be careful! . . . Don't pour too much wine at a time; amount will depend on the size of the macaroons. Mix with a fork until the texture is like a very thick mush. Let the mixture stand at room temperature. When it's dessert time, spoon **VANILLA ICE CREAM** into glass dishes and cover with this marvelous mix.

Lunch For Mr. Candid

. . . Easy there! He's so clever you'd better polish your wits as well as your silver

PORK CASSEROLE . . . He'll lick his chops over this one
You can cook this dish as early as you wish on Saturday morning. Buy 4 or 5 rather thinly sliced PORK CHOPS. Trim off fat around the edges and put some of it into your frypan to melt. When fat has liquefied, brown chops nicely on both sides. While they're browning and wafting a beautiful fragrance through your kitchen, peel 2 medium-size POTATOES and slice thinly. Do the same with 2 ONIONS separating the slices into rings. Slice ¼ pound of FRESH MUSHROOMS.

In your casserole, alternate layers of potatoes, onions and mushrooms. Cover all with a can of undiluted CONDENSED CREAM OF MUSHROOM SOUP. Sprinkle lightly with a touch of OREGANO, SALT and PEPPER. Top with pork chops and bake, covered, in a 350° oven for approximately 1 hour.

Serve the pork dish with a green salad or with Spicy Apples (right).

KEEP YOUR SALAD GREEN
An hour or two before he arrives, carefully wash and dry LETTUCE, CHICORY and ESCAROLE, or, if you prefer, WATERCRESS and pale ENDIVE. The greens will stay fresh in the crisper of your refrigerator as long as you leave them naked . . . without dressing. Just have OIL and VINEGAR cruets on the table. Pour on a bit of each, twist your PEPPER grinder, dash in some SALT and toss.

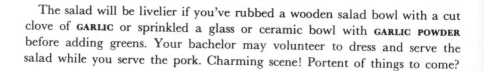

The salad will be livelier if you've rubbed a wooden salad bowl with a cut clove of GARLIC or sprinkled a glass or ceramic bowl with GARLIC POWDER before adding greens. Your bachelor may volunteer to dress and serve the salad while you serve the pork. Charming scene! Portent of things to come?

SPICY APPLES

Wash 4 or 5 APPLES and cut into quarters or eighths, removing core and seeds, but not peel. Place apples in a saucepan with 3 tablespoons of BROWN SUGAR, 1 teaspoon of CINNAMON and a few CLOVES. Pour in about an inch of any kind of FRUIT JUICE you happen to have, such as apple, orange or pineapple juice. Just don't use water. Add 1 tablespoon of LEMON JUICE.

Cover and cook over medium heat. Don't leave the room—at least not for long. When the apples begin to soften and break down, semi-mash them with a fork. Not too much—the consistency is more interesting when chunky and not smooth. Turn off the heat, leave the cover on and forget. Don't refrigerate. These apples are best hot, warm or at room temperature. Serve the sauce surrounded with KUMQUATS, which you can buy in a can or jar. When you set the table, be sure to remember small bowls for this fabulous fruit. The pork needs a plate all its own.

CHEESE AND CRACKERS . . . Simple sophistication

With a meal so rich, the dessert should be simple. Most men like CHEESE, so offer him several kinds. Remember to take the cheese out of the refrigerator about 2 hours before lunch; cheese should never be served cold. The CRACKERS should not be salty; they should have a delicate flavor so the full goodness of the cheese can be savored.

Be choosy about the cheese. Go international with PORT SALUT OR CAMEMBERT from France, semi-soft, mild to robust in flavor; GRUYÈRE from Switzerland, firm and nutty; EDAM from Holland, mellow as a cello; STILTON from England, milder than most blue-veined cheeses or go wild with sharpie LIMBURGER from Belgium. Or stay in the USA with LIEDERKRANZ, the mild man's limburger, or sharp CHEDDAR. In case he likes fruit with cheese, decorate your table with a bowl of FRESH FRUIT (no apples). For an added touch, serve a dessert wine.

Late-Night Suppers

or how to watch his wallet in style

You've had a perfectly lovely time crying all the way through a movie and, in the harsh glare of the lobby, he asks ever so compassionately where you'd like to go for a bite to eat. That's your cue. Pull yourself together and be generously womanly. As if the thought had just occurred to you, suggest casually that it might be nice to skip the bright lights and confusion and go to your place.

It's a chance he'll jump at and the opportunity you've been waiting for . . . to show your due consideration for the wallet that's paid for all those dinner checks, theater tickets and flowers.

Of course, what sounds like a spur-of-the-moment invitation to him has been well thought out and well planned by you—well in advance of the evening itself. But he'll never suspect. For him, it's an impromptu curtain call of the evening, and you're the superstar.

WELSH RABBIT . . . Not Rarebit

No matter what your bachelor or anyone else says, it is *Welsh Rabbit,* not *Rarebit.* Seems that in those long-gone days around Shakespeare's time, only the wealthy Welshman could afford to eat game. And the game little rabbit was a rarity; the poorer classes had to be satisfied with a game-less melted cheese substitute. So—an Elizabethan jokester called the popular dish a "Welsh Rabbit." End of history lesson—back to cooking class.

Invite him to come along to the kitchen and make the TOAST while you melt the cheese. In the top of your double boiler over hot but not quite boiling water, melt 1 tablespoon of BUTTER OR MARGARINE and at least ¼ pound of SHARP CHEDDAR CHEESE, cut into small bits. Stir until cheese melts. Continue stirring and add ½ teaspoon of WORCESTERSHIRE SAUCE, a pinch of DRY MUSTARD, a smidge of SALT and 1 beaten EGG. When all is smooth, slowly stir in ¼ cup of BEER. (Serve the rest of the beer with the rabbit.)

Pour the melted cheese mixture over the hot toast, which we trust he has ready. If you're hungry enough for something extra, add a few strips of crisp BACON. And if he's not a beer man, serve the royal rabbit MILK instead.

AVOCADO AND SHRIMP WITH A TEXAS TWANG

Cut a large *ripe* AVOCADO in half the long way and remove the pit. Place the pit, pointed end up, in water and keep in a dark, warm place. When it roots, plant in a pot of soil and raise a tree in your living room. But back to the ranch . . . Scoop out the fruit of the avocado; be careful not to tear the skin because you are going to fill the shells later. Put scooped-out avocado in a bowl and squeeze half a LEMON over it.

Chop 1 large TOMATO, 1 small ONION and 1 clove of GARLIC into the smallest possible bits. Add to avocado with a scant tablespoon of VEGETABLE OIL, a smidge of CAYENNE PEPPER, 2 teaspoons of CHILI POWDER and SALT as you wish. Mash all this together until smooth or, if you wish, use your blender.

Use two 4-ounce cans of tiny SHRIMP or cook a 10- or 12-ounce package of medium-size frozen shrimp, or start from scratch and cook and clean your own. When shrimp are cool, combine with the avocado mix. Spoon mixture into avocado shells and serve with CORN CHIPS for a super-snappy supper.

The avocado mix without the shrimp is Guacamole—a very good appetizer on its own or a perfect dripless dip for cocktail parties. Either way, it's superb.

LIVELY CHILI . . . Always rates a star billing

Buy 1 pound of LEAN CHUCK and have it ground. Adding nothing but your loving touch, form into very small meatballs, no larger than a marble. With about 2 teaspoons of VEGETABLE OIL in your frypan, brown the meatballs on all sides. Delicious juices will ooze from the meat as it cooks. When they're brown, transfer meatballs to a deep saucepan.

Meanwhile, with one eye on them and the other on your chopping board, cut up 2 medium-to-large ONIONS and 1 large GREEN PEPPER. Pieces should be about the size of your thumbnail. Chop fine at least 3 cloves of GARLIC. Add this flavorsome trio to the meat juices in the frypan and cook a few minutes, until wilted. Next, add 2 large TOMATOES, cut up, or a 1-pound can. Now, the seasonings! CHILI POWDER, of course; start with 2 teaspoonfuls. Then add ½ teaspoon of whole CUMIN SEED, SALT as you wish, a few strong twists of the PEPPER grinder . . . and your creative work is finished.

Add contents of frypan to the meatballs in the saucepan. Mix and set on a back burner over low heat to simmer for at least an hour (longer, if you have the time). Add a 1-pound can of RED KIDNEY BEANS, drained or with the liquid; remove from the heat to cool. Then into the refrigerator for at least a day—the taste improves tremendously with time.

You can make this chili some solitary evening when you're curled up with a book or burning up the telephone wires with him. After the movies, just heat it up. While waiting for the temperature of the chili to rise, chop a small ONION very fine, and grate some PARMESAN CHEESE in your faithful blender. Put each in an attractive small bowl, ready to be sprinkled on the chili at the table. The only other accompaniments you need are CRACKERS OR CORN CHIPS and COLD WATER (in case you've gone wild with the seasonings).

This recipe will serve two hungry couples very nicely if you are double dating. If not, don't worry. He'll surely want a second helping, and you can refrigerate the rest. It will keep well for at least a week.

FRUITED POUNDCAKE . . . A parting sweetness
Before you go out, cut up a mélange of **FRESH FRUIT**. Pour **ORANGE JUICE, KIRSCH, CHERRY HEERING OR SHERRY** over it and refrigerate. While you're at the movies, the fruit will be soaking up a lovely foreign flavor to add to its own natural goodness.

When you get home, toast slices of plain **POUND CAKE** until golden brown. Generously top toasted cake with the fruit—and a scoop of **ICE CREAM**, if you wish. Serve with **COFFEE**. He doesn't drink coffee at night? There's nothing wrong with **TEA** unless you make it with a tea bag he can see. Brew really good tea in a proper teapot; when you put in the tea, add a few **WHOLE CLOVES** for spice and something extra nice.

DATE–NUT DELIGHT . . . A smooth goodnight
Stew some **DRIED APRICOTS** before your date, or days before. (They're good with breakfast cereal or as a simple dessert.) Buy sliced **DATE–NUT BREAD**, a 3-ounce package of **CREAM CHEESE** and some **CHOPPED NUTS**. Soften cheese at room temperature and mix in 2 tablespoons of nuts. Spread mixture generously on bread. Top each slice with a spoonful of drained apricots. Serve 2 slices to each of you. Soooo good!

GINGERBREAD 'N' HOT APPLESAUCE . . . A warm farewell
Use store-bought **GINGERBREAD** or bake with a mix. Buy a 13-ounce jar of **APPLESAUCE**, and mix with a heaping tablespoon of **ORANGE MARMALADE**, a generous sprinkling of **CINNAMON**, a scant touch of **NUTMEG**. Heat the applesauce mix and heap onto slices of gingerbread . . . then add a dollop of **SOUR CREAM** for a really dreamy dessert.

"Impromptu" Dinners à Deux

or how to be clever and quick in the kitchen

One of these days you'll meet him quite unexpectedly (anyway, that's how it's supposed to look!). Suddenly the inspiration hits you and you ask him to dinner at your place. Do it! Just like that! No fussing; no planning. Or so it should seem. Chances are he'll accept just like that, too!

Surprise, not to mention variety, is the spice of life; the unexpected date is often far more fun than the evening you plan and look forward to for weeks or days. Serve him one of these plan-ahead, easy-do meals and he'll conclude you'd be so nice to come home to.

Or maybe you really haven't had a minute to do any advance cooking *or* planning, so serve him a truly spur-of-the-moment concoction. To be well prepared for impromptu or jiffy meals, have your kitchen shelves and refrigerator amply stocked with foods that keep well.

TUNA CASSEROLE . . . Quick as a wink

From your shelf of staples, take a 6- or 7-ounce can of TUNA FISH, a 2-ounce can of MUSHROOMS, a 4-ounce can of little WHITE POTATOES and some SEASONED BREAD CRUMBS; from the refrigerator, a wedge of CHEDDAR CHEESE, MILK OR CREAM and about 2 tablespoons of BUTTER OR MARGARINE. Slice 1 medium-size ONION and separate into rings. Slice potatoes if they are whole. Slice the mushrooms. Cut cheese into bits until you have about a cup.

Lightly grease your casserole with butter and layer by layer add all ingredients, dotting butter here and there and saving some crumbs and cheese for the top. Pour in ½ cup of cream or milk and it's off to a 300° oven until the cheese is melted and all is bubbly. Your very tasty spur-of-the-moment meal is ready.

CITRUS-ONION SALAD . . . The sweet and the sublime

This one's as enjoyable as a vacation in Florida. Simply peel 1 or 2 FRESH ORANGES and a GRAPEFRUIT. Separate into sections and spark with thin rings of RED ITALIAN ONIONS. Dress with OIL and VINEGAR.

The LAZY GARLIC BREAD (page 25) would be nice with this meal, and that's all you need except for a dazzling dessert. Read on.

RUM-BAKED BANANAS . . . A walk on the warm side

Peel and halve 2 almost-ripe BANANAS lengthwise. Melt 2 tablespoons of BUTTER OR MARGARINE and pour into a shallow bake-and-serve dish. Place bananas in the butter and bake at 400° for about 15 minutes.

Sprinkle a generous amount of BROWN SUGAR over the bananas and return to the oven for another minute or so until sugar blends with the butter and oozes deliciously over the fruit. Then pour about an ounce of RUM over the bananas. Your sinfully sweet dessert is ready to serve—or it can wait on your hot tray.

BEEF AND PASTA CASSEROLE . . . It isn't lasagne, but it's molto delizioso

Ask the butcher to grind 1 pound of **LEAN CHUCK**. Chop 1 **ONION** and mince 2 cloves of **GARLIC**. With your frypan lightly coated with **VEGETABLE OIL**, wilt the onion and garlic; remove from pan. Add a little more oil and cook the ground meat until brown, separating with a fork as it cooks. Return vegetables to the pan and mix together with the meat.

Cut up enough **CHEDDAR OR PARMESAN CHEESE** to make 1 cup. Cook about 3 ounces of **BROAD NOODLES** as directed on the package. Lightly grease your casserole and spoon in a layer of noodles, a layer of meat mixture, a sprinkling of cheese and **OREGANO**. Repeat until all ingredients are used. Over the dish pour most or all of a 14-ounce jar of your favorite prepared **SPAGHETTI SAUCE**. Bake about 30 minutes in a 350° oven until the cheese is melted. This recipe makes more than enough for two, but surely you'll both want second helpings!

Serve with **BREADSTICKS** and a crisp **GREEN SALAD**, dressed with **OIL** and **VINEGAR** or your favorite bottled salad dressing—maybe Italian?

ZABAIONE OR ZABAGLIONE . . . Easier to cook than spell

You can add several more letters to the spelling and create a great fuss over the cooking, but we think you should approach this great Italian dessert quite casually. Let your special guest watch as you take 3 **EGGS** and separate them carefully. Plop the yolks in top of the double boiler (over boiling water). Beat with your rotary beater, gradually adding 2 tablespoons of **SUGAR**. Keep beating until the yolks froth in the pan. Slowly add 3 tablespoons of **SHERRY, MARSALA OR BRANDY** while you beat the mixture very fast. (Refrigerate the egg whites, and make **MERINGUE KISSES** on page 53 another day.)

The egg yolks should not boil but must become thick and bubbly as you continue to beat, so don't stop for a second. When the mixture does thicken and bubble, your dessert is finished. It's lovely served hot, but if you don't want an audience, make it ahead and serve cooled in sherbet dishes.

OFF-THE-CUFF STROGANOFF

Never say *"nyet"* to Beef Stroganoff. All you do is buy 1-pound of tender **BONELESS BEEF SIRLOIN** and have it sliced very thin. Cut the slices into strips about 2 inches long and ¼ inch wide. Cut 3 or 4 **SCALLIONS** into tiny bits. Thinly slice about ¼ pound of **FRESH MUSHROOMS** or use a 4-ounce can. Mince a clove of **GARLIC**.

Melt 2 tablespoons of **BUTTER OR MARGARINE** in your frypan. When it's very hot, quickly sear the meat. Remove meat from pan and add scallions, mushrooms and garlic. Cook for a few minutes until tender. Add 2 ounces of **SHERRY OR DRY WHITE WINE**; mix well. Add about ½ cup of **SOUR CREAM** and mix again. Return meat to the mixture and heat quickly. Do not boil. Serve with **NOODLES**, cooked according to package directions, and top with **BROWNED BUTTER** and minced **FRESH PARSLEY**. On a platter, surround the Stroganoff with the noodles or vice versa.

SUPER SALAD

Make your usual great **GREEN SALAD**. If you have a **HARD-COOKED EGG**, slice and add to greens. Or, thickly slice ripe **TOMATOES** and dress with nothing but minced **FRESH BASIL OR CHIVES**.

Or, if you prefer, here are 2 dressings that will make you the winner of the chef's chapeau: **BLUE CHEESE DRESSING**—Into ½ cup of **SOUR CREAM**, mash or crumble a 2-inch square of **BLUE CHEESE, ROQUEFORT OR GORGONZOLA** (the flavor of all blue-veined cheeses is similar). Add 1 tablespoon of **LEMON JUICE** and a dash of **SALT**. Mix and you'll have plenty of this gorgeous dressing for the two of you.

CHILI-BACON DRESSING—Crisply fry and crumble into bits 3 slices of **LEAN BACON**. Toss bacon bits into ½ cup of **SOUR CREAM**. Add 2 tablespoons **CHILI SAUCE** plus a dash of **SALT** and **PEPPER**; mix. Serve on crisp salad greens or a wedge of **ICEBERG LETTUCE**.

CREATIVE CRÊPES

There are so many kinds of crêpes . . . some with just a little egg, some mostly egg; ours are entirely egg. Break 2 EGGS into a bowl. Thin with a tablespoon of MILK and beat with a fork. Melt 1 tablespoon of BUTTER in a medium-size frypan. Pour in half the egg mixture quickly, jogging the pan until the egg forms an even pancake. Cook quickly, being careful not to tear crêpe when you turn it. Slide out of pan.

Spread with APRICOT JAM and roll until crêpe is about 2 inches wide. Sprinkle with SUGAR. Repeat process with the rest of the egg mixture. Run both crêpes under the broiler for a few seconds until sugar forms a glaze. There's your dinner, all ready to be served from your hot tray with elegance and ease.

His Birthday Party

or how nice to burn the candle together

It doesn't matter whether he's 24 or 44, a man secretly loves being fussed over on his birthday. Invite him to dine on his natal day, and the glow in his heart will surely match the candle glow on his birthday cake.

If he's a globe-trotting man, the foreign accent of these entrees may be your passport to pleasing him. We've included Italian, French and Chinese-type main dishes—one of these may be a favorite of his. If you do happen to know his favorites, by all means build your menu around them. Maybe you know which dress is his favorite, too—wear that and show him just how thoughtful you are. And, after all, who knows? . . . This gala evening could well be the gentle nudge he needs to invite you on a global honeymoon!

CHICKEN ITALIANA

Select enough CHICKEN PIECES for two: legs, thighs, breasts or some of each. Brown them carefully in your frypan in about ¼ cup of VEGETABLE OIL. While this is going on, chop 1 large ONION, 1 GREEN PEPPER, 1 or 2 stalks of CELERY and mince 3 cloves of GARLIC. When chicken is brown, remove from pan; add the vegetables and cook until they are just wilted. Return chicken to pan.

Pour an 8-ounce can of STEWED TOMATOES over chicken and sprinkle with ½ teaspoon of OREGANO. Twist your PEPPER grinder over the pan a few times. Cover and simmer slowly for about 45 minutes, peeking now and then to make sure everything is nice and juicy. Add about ¼ cup of SHERRY and cook a few more minutes.

If the chicken is young enough, the dish is long since done. (Test by cutting off a small piece and tasting. Ready?) Place chicken on a platter. Surround with RICE, cooked according to package directions, but use CHICKEN BOUILLON instead of water. Pour sauce over chicken and if some dribbles on the rice, don't worry. That's the purpose of the rice . . . to give this gorgeous sauce something to cuddle up to. Serve with a crisp GREEN SALAD and dessert.

A "VERY RUM" CAKE

Buy a nice plain POUND CAKE, a small jar of NESSELRODE and a 4-ounce package of VANILLA PUDDING. Cook pudding as the package commands. Cut the cake in half lengthwise. Place bottom half on a serving plate and spread generously with Nesselrode. Place upper level back where it belongs. Spread more Nesselrode on top, and top that with a thick layer of vanilla pudding. Next, whip ½ cup of WHIPPING CREAM and top the pudding with it. Slowly drizzle about ½ cup of RUM over the cake to moisten. Refrigerate the dessert. Before serving you may want to add more rum, and, of course, you must put a candle in the center of cake and light it. Ask the birthday boy to cut or spoon the cake onto dessert plates.

NUTTY CHICK, CHINESE STYLE

This chicken is duck soup to make and takes only about 30 minutes. You need about ½ cup of raw ENGLISH WALNUTS OR ALMONDS; it's best to buy the nuts unshelled and crack them yourself. Boil about 2 cups of WATER with ½ teaspoon of SALT. Toss in nuts and boil for about 6 minutes; drain and cool. With your fingers, remove skins. Heat enough VEGETABLE OIL to cover the blanched nuts and carefully fry over medium heat until slightly brown. Remove nuts to paper towels and let cool.

Cut 2 CHICKEN BREASTS, skinned and boned (or use thighs or legs), into bitesize pieces. Chop 1 large ONION and 1 GREEN PEPPER into pieces about the size of a dime, and, if you wish, mince 2 cloves of GARLIC. Place chicken in a mixing bowl with 1 tablespoon of CORNSTARCH, 3 tablespoons of SOY SAUCE and 1½ tablespoons of SHERRY; mix very well.

Reheat some of the oil left in your frypan from the nuts. Toss in the chicken mixture. Fry over high heat for about 4 minutes, stirring constantly. Remove chicken. Add more oil if necessary and cook onion, green pepper and garlic for about 2 minutes. Add 1 tablespoon of SOY SAUCE and 1 teaspoon of SUGAR; mix well. Now add the chicken and nuts; stir and fry for about 1 more minute . . . and your dish is delicious. Serve with RICE.

FRUIT DESSERT . . . Kindles the flame of affection

Cut fresh, crisp fruits (maybe PINEAPPLE, APPLES and PEARS) into bite-size chunks. Arrange on a decorative plate with a chunk of BANANA in the center and KUMQUATS (out of a can or jar) around the outer edge. Drizzle LEMON OR ORANGE JUICE over the fruit to prevent discoloring and to enhance the flavor. Put a candle in the banana and light it.

When he's blown out the candle and made a wish, spear pieces of fruit from the serving plate with colorful plastic picks. Don't use individual dishes. Serve with FORTUNE COOKIES.

LE STEAK HOT, FRENCH STYLE

Buy 1 pound of sure-to-be-tender **BONELESS SIRLOIN STEAK**. Put some **BLACK PEPPERCORNS** (enough to make about a tablespoon when crushed) into a plastic bag and, with a small hammer, crush them coarsely. Your pepper grinder can't do the job this time . . . the pepper should be in small chunks. Press pepper into both sides of steak.

Melt 2 tablespoons of **BUTTER OR MARGARINE** in your frypan. Over a high heat, sear steak quickly on both sides. We hope you like it rare—takes less time, tastes more delicious. Remove steak and keep it warm. Pour 1½ ounces of **COGNAC**, ½ cup of **BEEF STOCK** and 3 tablespoons of **HEAVY CREAM** into the pan. Swish around over high heat for a few minutes. Add another teaspoon of **BUTTER OR MARGARINE** and quickly pour this savvy sauce over steak.

POTATO BALLS . . . Round out the steak

Before you cook steak, peel 2 medium-size POTATOES, cut into quarters and cook in 1 cup or more of BEEF BOUILLON. Meanwhile, chop 1 medium-size ONION and a few FRESH MUSHROOMS . . . and brown in BUTTER OR MARGARINE. When potatoes are tender, mash with BUTTER and MILK; add the browned onions and mushrooms. Mix all very well, and quickly form into little balls. When your steak's on the platter, circle it with the potato balls, and deliver posthaste to the table.

If he's a real baked-potato fan, have those instead. Serve with plenty of butter, sour cream and chives on the side.

ASPARAGUS-ALMOND TWOSOME

Wash 8 or more stalks of FRESH ASPARAGUS. Snap off the tough part, usually 2 or 3 inches of the stalk. Cut what's left into lengths of about 2 inches. Heat 2 tablespoons of VEGETABLE OIL OR MARGARINE in frypan. Add asparagus and cover. Cook over medium heat about 5 minutes and test for tenderness; don't overcook. When tender but not soggy, add a ½ cup of ALMONDS, cooked as in the NUTTY CHICK recipe on page 43.

If asparagus isn't in season on his birthday, have broccoli instead—the frozen spears are a snap to prepare.

A GREEN SALAD belongs with this meal. Before adding dressing, crumble in some ROQUEFORT CHEESE.

SPIKED PEARS . . . Add a little spice to his life

Buy 2 large PEARS, peel and leave them whole. Stud with WHOLE CLOVES every ½ inch or so. Heat 1 cup of BURGUNDY WINE and add ½ cup SUGAR, a CINNA-MON STICK or two and a sprinkling of NUTMEG, if you like it. Add the pears and cook at a leisurely pace until fruit is tender to the touch of a fork. Cool and serve with the mellow liquid. And don't forget to buy a BIRTHDAY CAKE.

Holiday Dinners

or how to hint about the good life in tandem

Holidays can be anything but jolly days for the bachelor. Of course he's invited to dinners—what bachelor isn't in demand? But unless he relishes other people's children climbing all over him, or listening to sisters and cousins and aunts who bear no relation to him, he probably wishes he'd sat the day out in solitude with a sandwich. And if you feel just about the same way, be different this year. Invite your bachelor to dine with you on Christmas, New Year's or any other holiday. Wear a festive daytime dress; and if you're so inclined, do something special with your hair. On Christmas, attach a big red bow at the back or scatter tiny red and green velvet bows here and there. Without saying a word, you'll be planting deep-rooted ideas about the happy family life.

Merry Christmas Meal

This menu is equally suitable for Thanksgiving, New Year's or any Sunday when you want to create a cozy family atmosphere with food.

ROCK CORNISH HEN . . . Live a little

Don't even think of roasting a turkey. Individual ROCK CORNISH HENS are much nicer and more practical for you—no long roasting, no tedious basting, no carving and no leftovers. Buy 2 small hens, about 1 pound each. Wash carefully and pat dry. Season inside and out with SALT and PEPPER—and a delicate sprinkling of GARLIC OR ONION POWDER, if you want some added zest. Put birds in a shallow pan.

Stuff each hen lightly with about ¼ cup of APPLE STUFFING (see next recipe) and sprinkle the entire bird with PAPRIKA. Melt about ¼ cup of BUTTER OR MARGARINE; pour over the birds. Roast hens in oven preheated to 350°. It will take about 1 hour to brown them beautifully.

APPLE STUFFING . . . Dress the bird in style

A fruit stuffing is more festive and just as easy to make as the usual bread mixture. Tear 4 slices of WHITE BREAD into bits. Chop 1 large or 2 small APPLES. Don't bother to peel them but be sure to remove seeds and core. Chop enough CELERY to make ½ cup, and do the same with an ONION.

Toss all with the bread pieces. SALT a bit, twist your PEPPER grinder a time or two, add 1 teaspoon of POULTRY SEASONING and about ¼ teaspoon of CINNAMON. Moisten mixture with 1 cup of CHICKEN BOUILLON (made with a cube and hot water). If stuffing is still dry, moisten with some WHITE WINE.

If any stuffing remains after filling the birds, form into little balls and roast them along with the hens. As a matter of fact, this stuffing is so good you may want to double the recipe; then you'll be sure to have plenty.

BARELY-COOKED PEAS
Buy a 10-ounce package of FROZEN PEAS and ¼ pound of FRESH MUSHROOMS. Wash the mushrooms and cut off the tough stem ends. Slice about ⅛ inch thick, keeping shape of mushroom. Place peas, mushrooms and 2 scant teaspoons of VEGETABLE OIL in a covered saucepan over very low heat. When the peas are defrosted and hot, the mushrooms will be finished, too, and the result sensational!

CRANBERRY-MARMALADE DUO . . . Sweet merger
Traditionally, cranberries belong with a Christmas meal. Yours are sweet 'n' easy. Open a 4-ounce can of the best brand of WHOLE CRANBERRIES you can buy. Mix with 2 generous tablespoons of good ORANGE MARMALADE. What a successful merger!

CHRISTMAS GREENERY SALAD
Wash, crisp and tear your favorite SALAD GREENS into bite-size pieces. Just before serving, dress them with this lightest of all dressings: 1 tablespoon *each* of WINE VINEGAR and WATER, ¼ teaspoon of GARLIC POWDER, 1 teaspoon of SUGAR, a generous sprinkling of OREGANO, several twists of the PEPPER grinder and a touch of SALT. Stir well. Pour over the greens and toss. This dressing is particularly light and perky because it has no oil—especially good here because it adds a refreshing touch to an otherwise rich meal.

WHITE CHRISTMAS DESSERT . . . Dream of a sweet
All you need is a pint of VANILLA ICE CREAM and a small bottle *each* of RED AND GREEN MARASCHINO CHERRIES. Put the ice cream in a bowl to soften. Meanwhile, chop about 10 cherries (five of each kind) into bits. Just before the ice cream turns to mush, stir in cherries. Spoon the merry mixture into a refrigerator tray and freeze. Serve in glass dishes with CHRISTMAS COOKIES.

Ask Him To Dinner on New Year's Day

Be brave: resolve to invite him to dinner on January 1st—
even though he may not be dating you on New Year's Eve . . .
even though he may be an ardent football fan from starting whistle to end.
Be smart: plan your dinner so he can arrive before game-time.
And serve at a table where the viewing is easy.
If that sounds like too much trouble or if you need time to muster your courage,
ask him for Easter dinner—this menu is just as traditional then.
As a matter of fact, it's suitable 'round the calendar.

ROAST PORK . . . Undeniable flavor power

A pork roast is the easiest and most delicious meat you can roast. Buy a 6-rib **PORK LOIN ROAST**, and ask the butcher to crack the bone (this will make the roast much easier to carve at the table). Peel a few cloves of **GARLIC** and slice as thin as you can. With your fingers and a small knife, insert these tiny slivers between the fat and the meat, here and there, all over the roast. If you hate garlic, don't use it—**SALT** and **PEPPER** are sufficient. But even that isn't necessary for the most delectable meat in the world. Place roast fat side up in uncovered roasting pan. Heat oven to 350° and allow 40 minutes of roasting time per pound. (Pork should be well done.)

When time is up, place this rapturous roast on a platter and surround it with canned spiced whole **CRAB APPLES** and/or **PICKLED PEACHES**—perhaps some **KUMQUATS**, too. Or, be traditional and serve applesauce; the few minutes it takes to warm it are well worthwhile.

If there's a chop or two left on the platter, you're in luck . . . you have the best part of a solitary meal on another day. Just reheat chop in the oven if the meat doesn't seem too dry. Otherwise, place in the top of a double boiler and steam the meat until warm.

SWEET POTATOES IN THE ROUND

Pare 2 large SWEET POTATOES OR YAMS and cut into slices about 1 inch thick. Pour a generous inch of ORANGE JUICE into a saucepan and add yams. Cover and cook until potatoes are soft to the light probing of a fork. But watch it! . . . don't let them burn. You may need more orange juice.

You can also mash the potatoes, put in a casserole dish and top with marshmallows. Place the dish in a 400° oven just until marshmallows brown.

ENDIVE OR "ONDEEV" . . . It's a great salad

However you pronounce it, BELGIAN ENDIVE is the perfect accompaniment to this meal. Buy two of the pale little stalks. Wash and cut off the bottoms that hold the slender, crisp leaves together. Separate leaves and place on salad or luncheon plates.

Crumble about ½ cup of BLUE OR ROQUEFORT CHEESE into ½ cup of SOUR CREAM. Add ½ teaspoon of WHITE VINEGAR. Mix and taste. If you want your dressing more piquant, add more vinegar. Serve the dressing in small oriental tea cups (without handles) if you have them—1 cup on each plate, with the endive. Dip leaves into the dressing and eat with your fingers.

LEMON MOUSSE . . . Just for the timid

Afraid to tackle a real mousse? Here's a respectable facsimile thereof. Cook a 4-ounce package of LEMON PIE FILLING according to directions on the package, but substitute ¼ cup of LEMON JUICE for part of the required water. Cool and refrigerate.

Beat the whites of 2 EGGS until stiff, gradually adding ¼ cup of SUGAR. Grate some LEMON PEEL until it bores you (about 1 lemon). When the lemon concoction is cold, fold in the stiffly beaten egg whites and grated lemon. Serve this mock mousse in a glass bowl, and, for a festive note, decorate it with canned MANDARIN ORANGE SEGMENTS.

Put Your Heart into Valentine's Day

Invite him to dinner on February 14th, but don't mention what day it is.
Just be your charming subtle self and he'll get the message.
The food you serve can be that unsigned communiqué you didn't mail.
As ever, all's fair in love and on St. Valentine's Day.

SPICY HEARTS . . . Tender loving trap

If you plan to serve cocktails before dinner, pass this conversation-provoking tray. Buy a jar or can of **MARINATED ARTICHOKE HEARTS** and some **SALAMI**, sliced thin enough so you can fold each slice in half. With your kitchen scissors, cut each slice into a heart shape. Place hearts on white **UNSALTED CRACKERS** which you've spread with just a touch of **MUSTARD OR MAYONNAISE** in the center (don't let it show). Spear each artichoke with a little pick and arrange them on a small plate. Place artichokes in the center of a tray and surround with your salami hearts on crackers.

SAY IT WITH ROAST BEEF . . . Words can't describe

Buy a small rolled **BONELESS BEEF ROAST**. Season with **SALT** and **PEPPER** or, if you wish, **GARLIC OR ONION SALT**. Place meat fat side up in uncovered roasting pan. Heat oven to 300° and cook according to the way he likes it—25 minutes per pound for rare, 30 minutes per pound for medium, 40 minutes per pound for well done.

If the two of you don't do away with the entire roast, you can make delicious **ROAST BEEF HASH** another day. Just brown chopped **ONIONS** and sliced canned **POTATOES** in a tablespoon of **VEGETABLE OIL**. Cube the leftover **BEEF** and toss into the pan. Season with a few drops of **WORCESTERSHIRE SAUCE** and cover. Let mixture sizzle a bit over medium heat . . . and that's it! Don't like hash? Then slice beef for scrumptious sandwiches or a snappy salad.

CHEESY POTATOES

Give the regal roast a companion in the oven. Pare 2 large POTATOES and slice them thin. Do the same with 1 large ONION, separating the slices into rings. Cut up enough SHARP CHEDDAR CHEESE to make about 1 cup. Alternate layers of the potatoes, onions and cheese in a slightly greased shallow baking dish. Sprinkle lightly with SALT. Cut 2 tablespoons of BUTTER OR MARGARINE into bits and scatter over dish. Lastly, pour about ½ inch of MILK OR CREAM into the dish, and bake for about 1 hour. Test potatoes with a fork; if finished earlier than the meat, rush to your hot tray.

LOVE APPLE SALAD . . The kind of valentine he likes

All you have to do is buy a container of CHERRY TOMATOES. Wash but leave stems on; serve on individual salad plates. In the center of each plate, sprinkle SALT and finely minced FRESH BASIL. If you can't buy basil, minced PARSLEY will do. Hold tomatoes by the stem and dip into salt-and-herb mix.

If you can't find cherry tomatoes, buy the full-size ones; slice thickly and serve on a bed of LETTUCE.

MERINGUE KISSES

If meringues had never been called kisses, we'd have invented the name for your Valentine dinner. Beat the whites of 2 EGGS and ⅛ teaspoon SALT until stiff but not dry. Slowly add ½ cup of SUGAR and continue beating until whites are stiff and shiny. Fold in ½ teaspoon of grated ORANGE OR LEMON PEEL.

Drop the meringue by the teaspoonful onto greased baking sheet. With the back of a spoon, hollow out a little well in the center of each meringue. Bake in a 250° oven for about 40 minutes. Cool and remove from pan. At dessert time, fill each meringue with ICE CREAM and crushed STRAWBERRIES, fresh or frozen. A kiss to remember!

Tricks Your Mother Never Taught You

* Solitary dishwashing is no torture. It's a time for meditating and making great decisions. It can even be fun if your bachelor offers to help. Otherwise, never wash dishes while your guest is with you. You'll diminish your graciousness with the clatter of crockery in the sink or the whirr of an electric dishwasher. Just stack and forget the dishes. Or walk away from the table grande-dame style. Clean up after he leaves and relive the evening as you swirl the dishes around in the suds. And, please, never wash even a few odds and ends between courses. If you don't have enough plates, spoons or whatever to get you through the meal, beg, borrow or give the dime store some business.

* Linen napkins are actually less expensive than paper. Good paper napkins cost pretty pennies and wind up in the garbage. But linen lasts, is so much nicer and looks lovely always . . . and really now, how long does it take to wash and iron a napkin? On the other hand, you'll need dozens and dozens of colorful paper napkins for your cocktail party. Warning! Beware of cotton napkins . . . some may leave lint on his suit.

* You don't need a multitude of pots, pans and sundry utensils to cook a fine meal. Here's a quick checklist: TWO FRYPANS, a medium-size and a large . . . THREE SAUCEPANS, a 2-cup size, and 2- and 3-quart sizes with covers . . . one shallow BAKE-AND-SERVE DISH . . . a 1½-quart CASSEROLE with cover . . . a medium-size ROASTING PAN . . . a BAKING SHEET . . . a couple of PIE PANS for a myriad of uses . . . a COLANDER for straining (be sure it stands on its own feet) . . . a DOUBLE BOILER (you can improvise this by nestling a smaller saucepan inside a larger one).

Or maybe your mother did teach you these tricks.
After all, she was a bright one
. . . she cooked her bachelor's goose
without this book!

Recipe Index